MW00413825

This book belongs to:

____

Made in the USA
Columbia, SC
01 December 2021

50207816R00061